Understanding The Outsourced Sales Professional

by Harold J. Novick

How manufacturers increase profits using manufacturers' agents

MANEF®

Manufacturers & Agents National Educational Foundation/
Manufacturers' Agents National Association

Novick, Harold J.
    Understanding The Outsourced Sales Professional / by Harold J. Novick

ISBN 0-9702694-0-4

Printed in the United States of America.

CONTENTS

FOREWORD

Ask any recent college graduate or even graduate student of business what their definition of a manufacturers' agent (or representative) is and you'll get either a blank stare or a rather vague description of a full-time employee of an enterprise that uses field sales personnel. This should not be surprising, as the profession has gone by a variety of descriptive, if not misleading, names over the past 100 years. These designations include manufacturers' agent, manufacturers' representative, sales agent, rep, broker, independent sales company, factory rep and a variety of combinations of these terms.

Most marketing, sales and sales management textbooks today devote little or no space to what has become the professional, outsourced field sales company. This is particularly disturbing in view of the fact that many texts written in the past decade deal extensively with the subject of outsourcing the non-core processes of a business. Even the government of the United States lacks a NAICS code to describe this type of business which boasts over 150,000 agents in North America and over 250,000 in Europe.

This grossly underestimated "channel" of distribution facilitates the field sales process that results in hundreds of billions of dollars in sales in the United States each year. According to the Electronic Representatives Association, annual electronics sales of $50 billion per year are handled by "independent" field sales companies in this industry alone.

In this book, Harold Novick does a masterful job of defining the professional manufacturers' agent and describes the advantages and disadvantages of this method of going to market. He also suggests the kinds of enterprises that might effectively use these independent sales agencies, and, in less than an evening's reading, prepares the business student to at least evaluate this method of mounting a field sales effort against the available alternatives.

While many manufacturers' agents will argue that neither their companies, nor their factory-employed counterparts are a "channel" in the sense that a distributor, dealer or value-added reseller is, the semantics here are less important than the basic principle. Simply put, the manufacturers' representative firm, whether it be a single-salesperson sole proprietorship or a corporate entity with 100 outside salespeople, is just one of the four ways that a manufacturer (or a service company) can choose to conduct field sales operations. Once a company decides that having off-site, face-to-face contact with customers is important, it can use non-sales employees of the firm, hire full-time factory salespeople, or employ an independent sales company that handles multiple, complementary, but not competing lines. Some companies will segment their markets or customers and employ a combination of these three methods.

Is field sales an anachronism today in this exciting world of e-business and technological change? I think not, at least in many B2B situations where the product is complex and/or technical, the sales dollar value of a particular customer is high or where customers desire suppliers who are strategic partners who can provide consultative services to them as well as products. As Novick points out, systems knowledge, knowledge of the customer's processes and personal relationships are more important today than ever. In these and other scenarios, we believe that field salespeople, rep or direct, and by whatever name or title, will continue to play an important part in world commerce.

In this work, Novick writes in the pragmatic style of one who has spent his career managing for-profit enterprises as well as in the academic world. His development of courses for the American Management Association and the University of Wisconsin lend credence to his expertise in this very important area. The student will come away with a good understanding of:

- What a manufacturers' agent is and is not.
- How major changes in customer organizations have changed their expectations of the salespeople who service them.
- The key characteristics needed in today's field sales forces, and how independent sales agencies often provide these characteristics.
- The advantages and disadvantages of selling through reps.
- Why some of the disadvantages are perception rather than reality and how many of the real disadvantages can be managed.
- The methodology to follow in developing an outsourced sales force.
- Techniques that result in success when managing independent field sales companies.

This is information that future business owners, sales managers and general managers need to have in order to help them evaluate the best way of going to market in their industries.

Bryant F. Callaghan
Chairman of the Board
Manufacturers' Agents National Association

INTRODUCTION

This booklet is about independent sales representatives, a sales channel that has become increasingly important to the producers of goods, systems and services worldwide and particularly in the United States. While the media focus has been on the emerging electronic world via E-commerce, E-trade, E-service and other electronic functions, major changes in customer organizations and customer expectations of their suppliers have made independent sales representatives the right channel alternative for thousands of companies, big and small.

The objective of this booklet is, therefore, to help the reader understand what independent sales reps are all about, why they are preferred to alternative channels in many scenarios and where they can be used to major advantage. An introduction to the operational aspects of managing independent sales representatives also will be presented.

This booklet is designed as an aid to the business student interested in a better understanding of alternative sales channels in the field of sales management. It is a complement to the many excellent texts on marketing and sales management that generally have not sufficiently addressed the role of the independent sales representative. For a more complete analysis of this critically important sales channel, the reader is directed to the book on the subject, *Selling Through Independent Reps*, Third Edition, 2000,

Harold J. Novick, published by the American Management Association, New York, New York.

We have presented material in this booklet as though it were addressed to a manufacturer or service provider. However, as any successful relationship between these two types of organizations and an independent sales representative must be based on a win-win situation, practices presented are also very pertinent from the sales representative's point of view.

SOME DEFINITIONS

Sales Channel — May be defined as the medium through which a supplier reaches its customers in order to sell its output, whether it be hardware, software, systems or other services. Sales channels include direct sales organizations, independent sales representatives, distributors, wholesalers, value-added resellers (VARs), E-commerce, telemarketing, direct mail and a host of others. While many companies may select a single channel through which to sell their products, more typically, a supplier will prosper by using hybrid channels, that is a combination of alternative channels to ensure that all market targets are properly reached. For example, a manufacturer may use direct sales personnel to solicit the major customers within a primary market target and independent sales representatives for secondary targets in the primary market and for secondary markets. Both may be complemented by E-trade, telemarketing and direct mail.

Other organizations may ladder their channels, that is using direct sales personnel or independent sales reps to sell through distributors and wholesalers who in turn may sell to third level distribution organizations before reaching the final buyer. Many variables affect the choice of channel. These include the size and complexity of the unit sale, the magnitude of the sales potential at given customers, technical complexity of the product, the array of support services required and the need for local service, to mention a few.

A Direct Sales Channel — A sales force made up of sales personnel who are directly employed by the supplier. Sales compensation for these personnel may be 100% salary, 100% incentive (i.e., commission) or various combinations of the two. Some companies call their sales personnel "independent" because their compensation is purely commission from which the sales personnel pay all expenses. If these individuals work only for this one company, they are defined as "direct," as they are economically dependent on only one company (i.e., employer).

Independent Sales Representative — A formalized sales organization of one or more individuals which contracts with suppliers to sell their products, systems or services, usually within a defined sales assignment, such as geography and market. (In this booklet, the term "rep" will be used for the full descriptive term.) Lines of different suppliers represented must be complementary and not competing. The primary differentiation between a direct salesperson and an independent sales rep is that the rep is under contract to sell the output of a number of suppliers. Compensation is typically 100% commission. The independent sales representative does not take title to the product or system produced by the companies they represent. They simply sell and take commission on the sale. While many reps are single-person organizations, one can find rep firms whose sales are in excess of $200 million annually with over 100 sales personnel. Puffer-Sweivan, the Houston representative for Fisher Controls, is such an example.

Agent — Generally, an agent is an alternative name for the independent sales representative. In a legal sense, an agent can bind their suppliers to a contract while an independent sales representative cannot. However, in practice, the two terms are synonymous in many industries.

Broker — In certain industries, brokers act exactly as an independent sales representative. Food brokers are one example. Their contracts will be very similar to that for independent sales reps except for the term broker rather than rep. Yet, the term broker is also used in other industries, such as in the securities industry and real estate, where brokers typically work for only one company. Other types of brokers may supply products from any number of manufacturers where they can find the best price.

Distributor — A distributor is also an independent sales organization, but one that will take title to a supplier's product or system, then resell it to end users or another independent organization in an overall distribution chain. Depending on the industry and distributor, competing manufacturers may be handled by a distributor. Another key aspect of distributors is their "value-added" capabilities. An example would be a distributor who assembles a number of products from different suppliers into a package that would then be sold under a single price contract to a customer.

The Rep-Distributor — While our definitions of reps and distributors define two different channels, the changing marketplace scenario has resulted in a major blurring of functional differences between the two. Based on the changing profiles of customers and their expectations of suppliers, reps in many industries have assumed various characteristics of distributors, buying select products, inventorying them, adding value and reselling products and systems to their customers as well as operating in the historic role of the independent sales representative. The role of the independent rep and distributor will continue to change as market conditions change. Therefore, when one looks at an "independent sales representative," one may readily find the firm performing any number of non-rep functions. As an example, upon examining the aforementioned Puffer-Sweivan, Fisher Controls' rep, one might ask the questions: Are they a rep? Are they a distributor? Are they a value-added reseller? Are they a service organization? The answer to all of the questions is "*Yes*"! Independent sales organizations, if they are truly growth oriented and customer sensitive, will sense changing customer needs and develop capabilities to satisfy these *local* needs typically better than any direct sales organization where macro solutions are typically mandated by the corporate headquarters.

Principal — The manufacturer or service provider under contract with an independent rep is commonly called a "principal" of the rep.

CHAPTER I

THE "INDEPENDENT" SALES REPRESENTATIVE

The introduction gave a brief definition of the independent sales representative, which we will refer to as rep or sales rep in this chapter, and the rest of the booklet. This chapter will further develop an understanding of the independent sales representative.

Figure 1, on page 16, presents a typical sales channel structure for business-to-business sales of products or services. Within this structure, there are several "levels of distribution," that is different steps in the movement of goods or services from the supplier to the end-user.

The first level of distribution is typically through a direct salesperson or an independent sales representative. The strengths and weaknesses of each will be given in Chapter III as will examples of their usage. This level of distribution is directly connected to the output of the manufacturer and can either sell this output to another level of distribution or directly to the end-user depending on the nature of goods and services provided.

The second level of distribution in this exhibit is the distributor. The first level serves the second level whereas the second level has a larger number of sales personnel covering a relatively small area to provide more intensive coverage than can otherwise be handled directly or through independent reps. Again, distributors will typically take title to the product, add value and resell and service the products. A pump manufacturer is a typical example. They may use direct sales personnel or reps as the first level. That level will then serve distributors who will inventory and resell pumps and pump systems to end-users, original equipment manufacturers, contractors and other resellers. In this scenario, rep personnel may call on end users to create demand and "pull sales through" distributor inventory.

When the product is of relatively small unit value and does not require a high level of technical support, third levels of distribution may be introduced, such as wholesaler, value-added reseller and jobber. Similar structures occur in the consumer products area, but with different name designations. It is beyond the scope of this book to discuss any of the second or third level distribution beyond this brief introduction.

Figure 1. Typical sales channels (industrial products).

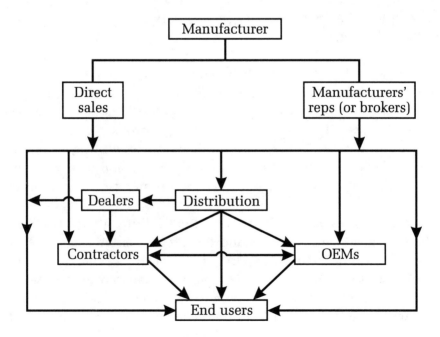

In selecting their channel or in evaluating their current channel, suppliers must evaluate their end-user targets with considerable circumspection. While the allure of E-trade is powerful and in many cases appropriate, there are countless products and services that require "touch" of customers by suppliers. This touch covers the range from complex problem solving for customers and helping customers understand complex technical proposals to simply providing the human contact that is so desirable when we are so heavily immersed in our increasingly electronic interfacing world.

The astute supplier will, therefore, frequently complement E-commerce with touch. To obtain a feeling for this need, readers should ask themselves the difference they have in reaction to receiving a telephone call from a computerized voice vs. a live person. To demonstrate this reaction, we ask attendees at our public seminars to advise what they do when they pick up a phone at home and hear a computerized voice. Almost without exception, the response is: "I immediately hang up." Then, we might go back to our laptop to continue reading E-mail, sending E-mail, loading a new program or proceeding on some other electronic venture. Thus is the love-hate relationship with the computer and why "touch" is so important.

Where do reps come from?

The founders of rep organizations are almost invariably spawned from supplier organizations. According to demographics published by MANA (Manufacturers' Agents National Association), the majority of founders were sales personnel, from direct salespersons up to national sales executives. Typically, they were top performers who were driven to become independent reps in order to obtain the benefits of independence, namely being their own boss and having the opportunity to earn significantly more money than they could as a salesperson in corporate life. While representing a much smaller percentage of the rep population, one can find former presidents, engineering managers and other top executives who become reps.

It takes a strong individual to leave the security of corporate life and become an entrepreneur, as is the case of every new rep. The rep who has excellent management capabilities as well as being a top sales performer is the individual who can build a really powerful rep organization, such as the Puffer-Sweiven organization previously mentioned.

The individuals starting a rep firm are typically in their early forties. At that point, they have already established a strong track record in corporate life and have assembled sufficient working capital to start their rep business. Then, depending on their managerial capability, market opportunities within their area and growth leaning, the owner may add sales personnel as rapidly as can be assimilated in the organization.

Typically, new reps start with only one primary manufacturer or service provider that will generate the major stream of income. As the founders do not have an established reputation, other suppliers they are able to attract may not be of top caliber and may not match the precise mix of products and services the rep wishes to offer. This is the lot of the new rep. Then, as the rep starts to establish the reputation as a top producer, their competence becomes notable in their industry. This attracts other top suppliers to the representative requesting that rep to sell their products and services in the territory. It may take five to 10 years before a high-powered rep truly assembles a mix of top manufacturers with the type of compatibility needed by that rep to serve those customers targeted by the rep and become "the best rep in the territory."

Reps are specialists

They'll specialize in one or more markets, a territory or even a group of customers. The business-to-business rep may also specialize in a technology. As a result of this specialization, reps will assemble a number of manufacturers and service providers that will allow them to present the whole portfolio of offerings to the same buyers and specifiers. The rep's objective then becomes to maximize the sales opportunities of their targeted markets and customers within their territory for the long term as well as the short term. It is this leveraging of compatible suppliers that is so important for a rep's growth and success.

Reps are really interdependent

While reps may be called independent, this is primarily in direct comparison to a direct salesperson who spends his or her full time selling for one manufacturer. Reps are truly not independent in the full sense of the term. Their success is heavily dependent on the manufacturers or service providers they represent and how well they serve these "principals." This is an important distinction, so much so, that one of the major rep associations, The Electronic Representatives Association (ERA) constantly stresses the fact that the relationship between manufacturer and rep is one of *"interdependence."* The professional representative (and the great majority of all independent reps are professionals) clearly recognizes interdependence and provides the manufacturers they represent with the degree of support as suggested by the relative financial importance of the manufacturer and the growth opportunities facing that manufacturer.

CHAPTER II

MARKET DEMANDS IN THE MILLENNIUM

A sales channel must be constantly examined in light of changing market demands and adjusted accordingly. There are many market factors that have influenced channel design through the end of the 1990s and will continue to do so into the millennium. Some have been essentially constant for 50 years, such as the need for ever-improving product quality. Others have been relatively new, as suppliers have undergone major changes through re-engineering, downsizing, acquisitions, product and technology expansions, and varying degrees of embracing E-commerce.

This chapter will present a number of key changes in the marketplace that require suppliers to rethink the characteristics that they need in their sales channels. They may be called megatrends in the marketplace.

Higher quality

In the mid 1970s, Japanese manufacturers were producing high quality products and making major inroads in U.S. markets with automobiles and electronic equipment. Many segments of American industry had failed to understand that the end-user wanted a quality product and would not be loyal to suppliers of inferior products. Thus, the American consumer started to buy higher quality Japanese cars and home electronics while industrial buyers looked to Japan for copiers, steel and miscellaneous other products. This was a loud awakening to American industry, which then committed to a long-term improvement of product quality in order not only to satisfy domestic needs but to become world-class suppliers.

Part of this transition was a major change in relationships with suppliers. For example, Xerox had some 5,000 suppliers of components for their office products in the 1980s. They concluded that the historic "buy from the low-price supplier" was not the best path to world-class quality. By the early 1990s, they reduced the number of suppliers to 300 and through the '90s reduced that level even lower. Xerox concluded that they needed the very best suppliers to help them design the best possible quality and value products for their customers. As a result, Xerox pre-selects a single preferred supplier to help them in the design stages of new equipment. The bottom line is that Xerox sharply improved their quality and assumed a world-class leadership once again.

What does this have to do with sales channels?

Well, suppliers who reach that precious acceptance with Xerox now have an exceptional amount of business being developed. On the other hand, over 90% of the prior suppliers no longer supply Xerox. They're on the outside looking in. The question now becomes: What can a supplier do to regain a position with Xerox and thus share in the much higher-volume potential for each supplier? Obviously, they must be world-class quality suppliers with the most current ISO quality systems and offer a great service package. Another key question is: "What type of salesperson do we need for Xerox to gain a position with them and where can we find that person?" Obviously, different characteristics are required for success with a Xerox-type customer. In an overall sense, the salesperson must help Xerox improve their profitability. A more detailed answer to this question will evolve over the ensuing two chapters. Chapter III will discuss characteristics needed in sales channels today. Chapter IV will discuss the pros and cons of direct selling vs. sales through independent reps in order to select a channel to best fit needed characteristics.

JIT deliveries — Just-In-Time deliveries are now the standard for a number of industries. This means that customers will not inventory large amounts of supplier parts but rather receive parts on the day, if not the hour, in which the part will be needed for the assembly line. This suggests there may be a need for the supplier to have a local inventory source to minimize shipment problems to satisfy their customer's JIT needs.

More assistance — Outsourcing by companies has been widespread for years. By outsourcing, we mean the elimination of in-house capabilities for manufacturing certain parts or providing certain services, such as engineering or financial services. For example, manufacturers such as DuPont have sharply reduced headquarters plant engineering capabilities and outsourced their engineering needs to consulting firms and suppliers. This literally means that supplier sales personnel must know more about customers' needs than many customer personnel in order to provide solutions for customer problems.

System supply — With the above downsizing of internal engineering support, customers are now more interested in a total system supply rather than individual pieces of hardware and software, which the buyer must then assemble into a system. This requires many hardware suppliers develop a systems supply capability or partner to offer systems solutions.

Lower prices — While improved product quality in the automotive industry has now been a 50-year trend, a newer trend, around since 1990, has been an enormous pressure on suppliers to reduce their prices. Demands are frequently placed on suppliers to reduce their prices by X% this year, Y% next year, and Z% the following year in order to obtain a three-year contract. This type of "partnering" has become widespread in many industries and we believe has been one of the significant factors in minimizing the degree of inflation the United States experienced through the end of the 1990s. It puts enormous pressures on suppliers to constantly reduce costs without sacrificing quality.

Increased concentration of purchasing power — In order to gain greater leverage over suppliers, customers have concentrated their purchasing power. This means converting local buying to centralized buying and even the creation of buying groups. However, branch locations may still have an influence on buying. Therefore, it does not mean the elimination of the need to contact local facilities as well as a centralized specification and purchasing function.

Customers reducing the number of suppliers — This is a reiteration of the Xerox example previously given. The trend sharply increased the value of a customer.

Increased computerization with an increased need for touch — Online procurement in general and certainly online releases from blanket purchase orders are standard in many industries. Computer interfacing between buyer and seller will further expand well into the millennium. However, it does not decrease the need for touch, i.e., face-to-face contact of a salesperson with customer personnel, even for commodity products when the sales potential of a customer is high.

Less available access to customer personnel — With the sharp retrenchment in staff support and downsizing of various service functions in customer organizations, existing customer personnel are increasingly unavailable to supplier sales personnel. This is almost contradictory as highly proficient sales personnel are needed more than ever by customers to serve their needs.

Voice messaging systems — These systems were originally designed to improve the efficiency of communications. Yet, they are now frequently being used to shield customer personnel from sales personnel.

CHAPTER III

KEY CHARACTERISTICS NEEDED FOR THE SALES FORCE

This chapter presents sales channel and sales personnel characteristics to satisfy scenarios presented in the previous chapter. Upon presenting each characteristic, we'll offer our feelings as to whether or not a direct sales channel or an independent sales force can best meet each characteristic. The opinions will not be based on the author alone. Rather, it's based on an overwhelming majority of opinions of attendees at our sales management seminar programs.

A complete understanding of customer needs

With the sharp reduction of customer support personnel, supplier sales personnel must have a complete understanding of customer needs in order to better service these customers.

> *Rep or Direct?* — Independent reps, as a general rule, are in a better position to understand customer needs because of a longer tenure they typically have with given customers. The objectives of the rep owners are long-term service to their customers. If they are also good managers, other sales personnel in the firm will also have the same objectives. The objectives of a direct salesperson are to be promoted out of their existing customer assignment and thus break the tenure and understanding of each customer's needs.

Systems rather than just product competence

Product knowledge was a primary characteristic historically for sales success. That has been superceded by the need for a salesperson to understand the complete system into which the product or service is to be integrated. When it comes to product knowledge, a direct salesperson usually has greater product confidence because of their concentrating full-time on the products of one manufacturer. Yet, today's market scenario has relegated product knowledge secondary to systems competence.

Rep or Direct? — Independent reps will assemble a number of products and services that are highly compatible. Together, they can comprise a complete system. This broader perspective means that the right independent rep will generally be in a better position to present systems offerings to customers than a direct person.

Consultative selling skills with alternative solutions

Customers want sales personnel calling on them to help them increase their company's profitability. This can normally be done through high-level, consultative selling with alternative solutions to help the customer arrive at the most cost-effective solution within financial parameters established by the customer.

Rep or Direct? — The rep again is in an inherently stronger position than all but the largest direct sales organizations because of their other lines and longer tenure with customers. The other lines offer alternative functional solutions with each solution fitting a special niche rather than being direct competitors. This typically places the rep in a more objective selling posture. For example, a part for a piece of machinery might be made as a casting, forging or a welded part. A rep with compatible principals could handle all these solutions and help the customer make the best selection comparing strength, durability, price and other factors.

Vertical market specialization

Summing up the ingredients of the aforementioned three characteristics, one can only conclude that sales personnel should now be vertical market specialists rather than product specialists serving all markets wherever economically possible.

> *Rep or Direct?* — Independent reps naturally gravitate to this specialization — at least in those trading areas where there are large concentrations of a targeted market. Conversely, it would be cost prohibitive for most manufacturers to attempt to develop this type of vertical specialization with a direct sales force.

Long-term continuity and acceptance with buyers and specifiers

This continuity and acceptance is required to allow the salesperson to develop and successfully manage the relationships between the company he or she represents and the customer.

> *Rep or Direct?* — As mentioned earlier, this continuity is inherently an advantage of independent sales representatives. They have a long-term, vested interest in a given market within a given territory. The interests of a direct salesperson are to get promoted out of that territory.

Ability to offer local solutions

Corporate planning invariably leads to macro solutions for market opportunities. The intent is to allocate resources wisely and only go after primary opportunities. This means that local needs, while real, may not be satisfied by such corporate decision making.

> *Rep or Direct?* — The evolving independent rep will fill in voids in one of their offerings by developing that capability themselves. A customer may want a product to be skid mounted but the supplier of the product chooses not to do so. The aggressive rep will arrange to subcontract the mounting and give the

customer what they want. The same will be true for any number of other services. A direct salesperson generally offers the macro solution from headquarters. The independent rep will develop flexibility to modify the macro offering to fit the micro need of specialized situations. This is one of the major reasons why Fisher Controls, whose sales are around $1 billion dollars in North America, still is committed to the use of reps.

Sufficient headcount to provide intensive coverage of all targeted markets

For companies that have multiple target markets, vertical market specialization and other sales force characteristics indicated above require a rather large headcount of sales personnel to provide required coverage.

Rep or Direct? — Direct personnel represent a semi-fixed cost. This is a large financial investment up front while waiting for sales results. The great majority of companies simply do not have the financial strength to develop such a sales structure. Independent sales reps, by the nature of their being compensated purely by commission and generally not being paid until either the product is shipped or paid for, allow the assembly of a large headcount series of sales channels that can provide intensive coverage to all targeted markets. While they represent other principals and may not present one or more of them on every sales call, each call further develops a relationship with the customer that can be productively used later.

Close physical proximity to customers

This is another high headcount need. Most customers prefer to have sales personnel who are local. The need of immediate response is more quickly satisfied by a local person than one who is a 1,000 miles away.

Rep or Direct? — An independent rep channel will be in much closer proximity to customers than a direct sales organization. Their multi-manufacturer line status affords much larger headcount with more local coverage than can be obtained in a direct sales force for all but the largest companies.

Computer literacy

The millennium will see an ever-increasing need for a salesperson to be thoroughly computer literate. This literacy will be the result of the manufacturer's rapid expansion of computer system interfacing between their company and suppliers for a wide array of functions including diagnostic tools, proposal presentations, JIT interfacing and troubleshooting, to name a few. In addition, the sales management function can improve sales effectiveness through a number of excellent contact management software programs that require routine inputs from sales personnel.

Rep or Direct? — A direct sales force is inherently in a much better position to satisfy a manufacturer's needs for computer literacy in its sales channel than an independent rep channel. The reason is simple. A direct salesperson spends 100% of his or her time for one manufacturer. The independent rep, on the other hand, must not only serve multiple manufacturers, they must serve the needs of their own organization. This introduces significant obstacles for one manufacturer to use all of the desired software programs throughout a rep channel. One exception would be where the manufacturer contributes the dominant share of a rep's income. This economic leverage minimizes, but still does not eliminate, the problem of software conformance with independent rep networks.

A variable expense

The need for a variable expense, that is, an expense that does not occur at least until a sales volume is reported on the P&L, becomes an economic imperative for the great majority of companies in the millennium market scenario. Vertical market specialization and the need for local support of customers with highly competent personnel require companies to use more sales personnel then ever before.

Rep or Direct? — Sales expense using an independent rep channel is a variable expense, that is, an expense that does not hit the P&L until sales for the contract obtained by the rep are reported on the P&L. A direct sales force represents a semi-fixed expense that is reported on P&L well in advance of the sale. This means that all but the largest companies will not be able to economically afford the type of channel dictated by the millennium market scenario in most industries.

CHAPTER IV

THE ADVANTAGES OF SELLING THROUGH INDEPENDENT REPS

This chapter summarizes the characteristics of independent representatives that offer advantages to manufacturers and service providers compared to direct selling. Caveats will also be noted where appropriate.

Selling in one territory is the rep's life

This long-term commitment leads to customer continuity, customer closeness, knowledge of customer processes and the ability to manage relationships between suppliers they represent and their customers. Obviously, not all reps have equal capability. It, therefore, becomes incumbent upon suppliers to find the best available rep in each territory and provide that rep with good support.

Synergistic principals

The well-managed rep will assemble a number of product and service providers (commonly known as "principals") that fit a strategic scheme to optimize their talents in selling to a defined market within their trading area. A proper array of principals will mean strong sales growth that in turn leads to:

- higher headcount with more selling hours available
- in-depth coverage of targeted markets

- the ability to offer systems solutions
- the ability to use advertising leads from one of their principals as leads for others they represent
- more objective feedback to each supplier they represent as a result of their broader perspective

Again, not all reps in a given area who could handle a manufacturer's product line have equal compatibility with that manufacturer. It, therefore, becomes critical for a manufacturer to conduct an in-depth analysis of their markets in order to determine what types of products and which manufacturer within each product class is most compatible with their own product line. By the term "compatible" we mean that the product or service is bought or specified by the same functional levels in customer organizations, is similar in terms of features-benefits-value-price, is used (or resold) by common individuals in the customer organization and, in the case of technical products, is installed on the same system. Finding the most compatible rep is one of the major challenges a manufacturer faces in becoming successful with reps.

One example of compatible lines would be a rep who handles capital and auxiliary equipment for the process industries. The rep who handles a reactor manufacturer may get involved in the construction of a new refinery at the early design stage with the consulting engineer. The reactor is a major piece of capital equipment that is designed into the early stages of a refinery. The rep then has the inside track to get other manufacturers that he represents specified. This could include heat exchangers, pumps, fabricated piping and other auxiliary (i.e., lower cost) products.

Willingness to supply solutions that satisfy local needs

Reps are highly sensitive to customer needs, as their long-term objectives hinge on satisfying those needs. If a manufacturer they represent has a shortfall in their offering, reps will typically rise to the occasion and find a local source to complete the manufacturer's offering.

Fast access to new or marginal markets

Recruiting a rep who is established in a market that is not currently penetrated by a manufacturer provides the contacts and influence with prospective customers that would be very difficult to do on a direct basis. The same is true with marginal markets where a direct person cannot afford to spend the necessary time. A rep, who is leveraged by other manufacturers' products, can afford the time necessary to develop strong relationships and convert those relationships to sales for each of the manufacturers they represent.

Financial advantages

Reps offer three financial advantages compared to direct sales forces. They are:

Variable expense — Reps are not paid until they perform, that is until they achieve the new orders. They are then not paid until either the product is shipped or until the supplier's invoice is paid (this depends on the industry standards for payment). As a result, the P&L is not impacted by selling expense until the sales are actually taken on the P&L.

Cash flow — It also means that cash flow is deferred until well after the desired event (getting the order) is achieved — at least compared to a direct sales force.

Balance sheet management — A newer advantage is balance sheet management. Reps have assumed significant distribution overtones over recent years to satisfy emerging customer needs. As a result, many items that would normally go on the supplier's balance sheet have now been purchased by the representative and moved to the rep's balance sheet for resale, e.g., spare parts.

A business advisory source

Successful reps are very sound business people. They are business unit managers of their own firm. Their perspective provides great insight in comparing suppliers they represent and in advising suppliers how they need to improve if they wish to achieve their objectives. They can be very effective advisors.

WHO SHOULD USE REPS?

As a result of these advantages, reps can be of significant advantage to companies of all sizes. Here are several different examples (more expanded information on these examples is presented in "Case Examples," Chapter VIII).

Large companies (sales in excess of $1 billion)

The aforementioned Fisher Controls has annual sales through independent reps in North America of nearly $1 billion and worldwide sales in excess of $1.25 billion. They are pre-eminent in their field of instrumentation and control with highly profitable returns. However, most billion-dollar companies are direct. Historically, the generally accepted notion about reps is that you use them when you're small but go direct when you're large. Fisher refutes this historic notion.

There is normally no absolute size at which a company should convert from rep to direct selling. The basic fact is that the more a manufacturer contributes to a rep's income, the more the rep assumes characteristics of a direct sales organization. In fact, John Weekley, former vice president of sales for Fisher Controls, referred to the Fisher rep sales force as a "pseudo-direct" sales force. This is the result of the commission income reps receive from Fisher averaging around 90 percent of their total income.

As an alternative channel strategy for large companies, Hewlett-Packard's medical products group offers an attractive channel strategy for rather large direct organizations. This is the use of independent reps to complement a direct sales force where direct selling is non-economical, namely to smaller accounts in a given industry or to marginal industries.

The medium-sized (i.e., over $100 million) company

Glegg Water Conditioning, Inc.[1] of Guelph, Ontario, Canada, is a great example of a company that started with reps in its infancy not many years ago and now is in excess of $100 million in annual sales. Still, they sell primarily through independent reps in North America. This company has capitalized on the inherent strengths of independent reps and developed a customer-oriented rep network to address customer needs in strategic industries. These separate rep channels were developed for the power, electronics and pharmaceutical industries.

Small companies

The smaller company, which we generally define as below $50 million in annual sales, is invariably better off selling through independent reps if they need wide geographic coverage in the United States, target multiple markets or a combination of the two. It is simply cost prohibitive to assemble a sufficiently large enough direct sales channel to provide such coverage, as the cost of a single direct salesperson including compensation, fringe expenses and other direct overhead frequently averages $150,000 per year or more.

---

[1] On October 15,1999, Glegg Water Conditioning, Inc. was purchased by General Electric. The acquired firm has been renamed GE-Glegg Water Technologies. In this booklet, the former name will be used.

CHAPTER V

DISADVANTAGES OF INDEPENDENT SALES REPRESENTATIVES

Corporations today outsource many functions including segments of engineering, manufacturing, finance and data processing. Selling through independent reps is no different. It is outsourcing the sales function and has been a practice since the early 1900s. If companies recognize that this outsourcing function is essentially establishing a partnership that must be mutually profitable and satisfactory, suppliers will receive some outstanding returns for their investment in an independent rep sales force. However, success will only be maximized by those companies who understand the trade-offs when selling through reps and learn to manage the independent nature of reps effectively.

This chapter is, therefore, devoted to disadvantages of selling through independent reps. It also demonstrates how these disadvantages can be managed in order that the needed advantages of the representatives can be optimized.

A more complex management job

Selling through independent reps is inherently more complex than selling direct because the reps do not devote full time to one supplier's products or services. Fortunately, this complexity is not severe, as the ingredients that make up the complexity are easy to understand as long as a partnership approach to the relationship is taken.

Little control

Managerial egos still have a propensity to direct subordinates rather than to manage them. If this propensity is directed at independent reps, it will be akin to shooting oneself in both feet before a race. Reps are reps because they want to be independent and partner with the suppliers they represent. Really successful reps, the ones that the suppliers need, will automatically shift attention away from any suppliers they represent who have dictatorial sales executives or presidents. Conversely, they will bend over backwards to support suppliers they represent if the supplier is well matched and if the management team of the supplier properly respects and supports the rep's activities.

The bottom line is that authoritative control is not the way to motivate any salesperson, whether direct or a rep. In the case of reps, it is a highly demotivating management style. The supplier's management team must, therefore, learn how to properly partner with their reps with the objective of achieving financial success for both partners.

Reps have a second set of competitors

This set is the other manufacturers they represent, as they compete for your rep's selling time. Fortunately, this is one of those cases where a disadvantage also offers a major advantage. The obvious advantage is the synergistic factor that a rep's other manufacturers or service providers have with your company. There is also another advantage. A supplier may be able to get more than a fair share of time from a rep if the supplier precisely fits the rep's needs and gives that rep outstanding support.

Reps may not divulge information needed by their suppliers

Unfair terminations of representatives by their suppliers have resulted in many rep owners keeping information about their company "close to their vest." This is contradictory to a top working relationship, as openness and candor are needed to maximize the profitability of the relationship for both partners. We would not recruit a representative who refuses to divulge needed information about the rep's firm in order to properly appraise the firm. Typical information needed by a supplier to evaluate a rep candidate includes the complete historical evolution of the firm, ownership, biographic sketches of all salespersons, support services, companies they represent, including a definition of the most important ones (particularly those that together contribute a great majority of the rep's income), how long each of the major principals has been represented, trading area that is intensively covered, how their sales are broken down by market target, who are the primary customers, what sales strategy drives the firm and the plan for continuity of the firm if the owners are near retirement age. Fortunately, we find that if one is very open in presentations to reps, reps are quite open in return.

Changing rep objectives

If there is one common characteristic of companies in general, it is that objectives will change as a function of time. Your company's objectives will change. The rep's objectives will change. This is a normal evolution. It may mean that at a point in time, the rep's objectives are no longer aligned with your company's objectives. At that time, the contract should be adjusted or terminated based on the severity of the diversity and on alternative solutions available.

Reps may stop selling for you, but not tell you

As a result of changing objectives, lack of support by your company or other factors, reps may stop selling for you, but not advise you of the fact. If the rep decides that you are no longer a principal that fits their plans, they may not terminate you, but simply accept the commission from residual business without proactive selling effort. It is, therefore, incumbent upon the supplier to keep relatively close contact with their reps so that such a reversal of commitment can be quickly defined, the reasons for same pinpointed and a decision made as to what course of action needs to be taken.

May not provide for continuity of the firm,
but just slow down and retire

Rep owners maybe segregated into two classes concerning the life cycle of their firm. One class would be those owners who reach a point in the aging process whereby growth is no longer important. Rather, a comfortable lifestyle becomes the imperative. As a result, there are no plans for continuity of the firm. In essence, the rep simply slows down and eventually retires. As an independent business owner, this is entirely within their rights. In these wind-down years, their sales typically plateau, then decay. Market share of the companies they represent, therefore, erodes.

This is an unacceptable scenario for any public corporation and for most privately held ones. Stockholders want growth. Any rep who opts for lifestyle rather than growth becomes an impediment to the company's success. Here's where delicate negotiations between the manufacturer and the rep may result in a win-win situation. It can be the result of the retiring rep developing a working relationship with another independent rep who would eventually take over the manufacturer's lines. Other alternatives could be a change in contract to a specific customer list or reduced territory with a new rep recruited for the needed additional coverage. If such negotiations are not fruitful, it may mean that the lifestyle rep should be terminated and a growth rep obtained.

The growth-oriented rep, on the other hand, develops continuity for his or her firm. This means ownership sharing with employees of the firm. Then, as the original owner reaches retirement age, a final buyout of the business between the founding owner and the new owners can result in strong continued growth of the firm.

May be poorly managed

The founder of a rep firm may be an outstanding salesperson but a poor manager. As a result, the firm is never able to attract and hold qualified sales personnel. These firms can be identified by turnover of companies represented and turnover of sales employees combined with their recruitment of lesser-qualified people. Reps of this type can typically be identified during the initial screening process and should be avoided.

May not be responsive to requests they consider superficial or bureaucratic

Reps are "doers" rather than planners and administrators. If they receive a request that they consider superficial or bureaucratic, response to the request will be highly uneven through a rep network. It is, therefore, imperative that a manufacturer recognizes this characteristic of independent reps and develop communications systems accordingly. This is particularly true relative to any desired reporting system. Reps handle a number of different manufacturers. It would simply be inefficient for them to respond to each reporting system desired by each manufacturer they represent. Reporting systems should, therefore, be simple and in many cases, should be verbal. Upon receiving the verbal input, the manufacturer may then reduce it to whatever internal reporting system is required. This is not a universal problem. A number of industries, particularly hi-tech, use reps who have superb reporting systems.

Difficult to obtain software conformity

This will be a continuing problem with the great majority of independent networks. The complexity is based on different manufacturers desiring different reporting systems and using different software systems. In addition, the acceptance and use of various software programs varies enormously from rep to rep. We have no simple answer for this issue and it represents one of the only significant disadvantages when using an independent rep network compared to direct selling.

You cannot fire one member of a rep firm

It is rare to find a multi-person rep firm where each individual has an equal commitment to each of the manufacturers represented. In fact, a manufacturer may find one member of a rep firm who does not spend any time selling for that manufacturer. If appeals to the rep owner fail, the manufacturer is then faced with few alternatives. The bottom line frequently is to accept the output that the rep firm gives you even though it is missing one individual or terminate the rep firm and search for a new firm.

Today's compatible manufacturer may be tomorrow's competitor

Two scenarios develop to present this problem. In one case, a manufacturer represented by your rep may bring out a product that directly competes with your product. If the other manufacturer has a much stronger financial position with the rep, it may result in your termination. An alternative scenario is one in which a competing manufacturer may acquire one of your rep's manufacturers and force this same situation. Both of these do not occur very frequently, but they do occur at times and are uncontrollable.

A more complex and chaotic management job

Selling through a direct sales organization is a much simpler management job than selling through independent representatives. The special considerations that we have listed prior to this statement indicate what the primary complexities are. Fortunately, most of them are controllable and are not major deciding factors in concluding whether or not your company should be using independent reps or direct sales personnel in all or in part. Today's marketing dynamics, as outlined in chapters I and II, clearly call for the advantage of using independent reps rather than direct sales organizations for most companies.

CHAPTER VI

DEVELOPING A STRONG
REP SALES FORCE

Careful planning is required to develop a high performance, independent rep sales force. Considerably more circumspection is required than if one were to be developing a direct sales force because of the independent nature of rep firms. Individuals become reps as a result of two primary motivations, namely they want to be their own boss and have no limitations on their income. This means that if a manufacturer or service provider is to have outstanding rep performance, they must select a rep that has essentially the same objectives as the manufacturer in terms of market targeting, market niching, technology and other factors. Owners of rep firms will build their business to satisfy their own needs. It, therefore, is incumbent to match these needs with a manufacturer's needs.

To achieve the preciseness of match between rep and manufacturer that leads to outstanding rep performance, two critical steps are needed in the search and selection process. These steps are:

1. Define a profile of the ideal rep
2. Design and implement a highly proactive rep search program.

This chapter will review the key ingredients for successfully completing the above steps.

THE IDEAL REP

As one cannot "control" an independent rep, it is imperative that the rep selected has characteristics that match what the manufacturer is all about as closely as possible. Essentially, the rep should be a mirror image of the manufacturer. Following are the primary characteristics a rep should have to be successful with the manufacturer:

Market mix

The rep firm's market mix should closely parallel that of the manufacturer. This means that the rep's business comes from those markets targeted by the manufacturer. For example, if a pressure vessel manufacturer (e.g., Buckeye Fabricating), were to target the wet process markets within the chemical process industries (CPI), the rep should also be primarily focused on wet process applications within the CPI.

This general market target compatibility must be further refined. If the manufacturer sells high-end, value-added equipment at high prices compared to competitors, the key decision makers at the customer levels may be the engineering department rather than the purchasing department. This means that the rep should be very engineering oriented and sell most of their product lines by gaining preferred specifications for high value products.

Let's now assume that the manufacturer of pressure vessels also builds tanks for the municipal waste treatment market. The ideal rep for covering the CPI may not call on the municipal market. If that is the case, the rep should be recruited for the CPI market only and a separate rep selected for the municipal market. As reps tend to specialize in markets, at least in trading areas where certain vertical markets have large potential, multiple reps may be required in a given area with each rep concentrating on a certain vertical market. It is this market specialization offered by independent reps that is so important in today's market conditions.

Compatible products

The rep should have product lines that are compatible with the manufacturer's products. In the case of a tank manufacturer, compatible products would include various wet chemical process equipment (e.g., mixers), liquid handling equipment (e.g., pumps), heat exchangers (air-liquid or liquid-liquid) and similar equipment. As mentioned earlier, if the manufacturer seeking the rep is "high end," that is, offering products with features, benefits, value added and high price, manufacturers represented by the rep should be of a similar characteristic. This will help assure the rep not only knows how to sell high-end products and systems but also sells to those customer functions which influence the purchase.

Sales personnel

Rep sales personnel should have a sound track record of successfully selling compatible and/or competing products into the manufacturer's targeted markets within the territory in which the rep is to be selected. Typically, we would look for a rep firm whose sales personnel average at least 10 years of such experience.

No directly competing manufacturers

This is a given in the rep-manufacturer relationship. A condition of the contract should be that the rep does not handle directly competing lines, that is, manufacturers of products that are direct substitutes for all applications targeted by the manufacturer. On the other hand, a rep who handles "functionally competing" lines may offer the manufacturer an advantage. By the term "functionally competing," we mean a product that can do essentially the same job as the manufacturer but does it in a different design fashion and really serves a niche that is different from the manufacturer's niche. Representing such product lines allows the rep to be in the most objective posture possible in presenting alternative solutions to a customer and recommending which solution is best. Obviously, considerable thought must be given to the functionally competing manufacturer and the rep's relationship to that company. If the functional competitor is the top income producer for the rep, that rep may be biased towards presenting the functional competitor rather than the new manufacturer.

Good tenure with top manufacturers and qualified personnel

Probably the best indicator that a rep is an outstanding performer is their ability to attract and retain top manufacturers in their product class and highly qualified sales personnel. Obviously, these characteristics can only be evidenced by a rep who has been in business for a considerable period of time, say 10 years or more. The rep owner, if he or she is also a top manager, will develop such tenure, as the need to attract and hold highly qualified sales personnel is mandatory if the firm is to attract and hold top manufacturers.

Interest in representing the manufacturer

The rep should show an enthusiastic interest in representing the manufacturer. At times we have observed manufacturers who kept on pestering a rep over a long period of time until the rep finally said: "Okay, we'll give your company a try." This is not the way to start a relationship with a rep. The relationship should be based on equal need and interest if a manufacturer is to have the highest possibility of success with the rep.

The above characteristics tend to be the most important ones in recruiting a rep. However, there are a number of other characteristics that are attractive but not necessarily the most important. The reason for separating characteristics into at least two priorities is to make sure that a manufacturer focuses on the most important characteristics a rep has if they are to be highly successful with that manufacturer.

Secondary characteristics of interest are:

Tenure of the firm — A rep firm which has been in business for 10, 15 or more years develops an excellent reputation in the area. However, this is of secondary importance to the strength of the individuals who are selling in the firm. For example, a rep may be newly formed but with five or six top sales personnel who resigned from another rep to start their new firm. The firm itself does not have an established name but the sales personnel do.

Growth driven — At times this could be a primary characteristic, but for most companies who have little business in a targeted area, the more important characteristic is that the firm is very well established in the area. The firm may comprise senior personnel with ages from 50 to 70. Growth may no longer be the drive of the owners, but their existing sales volume and their outstanding contacts can help a manufacturer quickly gain market share. Growth may well be sustainable for five, 10 or more years before a replacement may be required.

A balance of headcount and principals within the trading area — Ideally, the rep firm should have ample headcount compared to the number and size of principals represented. Age spread of the firm's members should ideally range from the senior salesperson who has long-term established contacts at senior decision-making levels to young personnel who have strong academic qualifications and the dedication to grow into top sales performers. The younger personnel are actually better equipped to open new accounts as the senior people may well have little interest in going into prospects where they are not currently well received.

Product experience — Rep sales personnel should have a certain level of sales experience with the manufacturer's type of products. However, this is entirely secondary to the need that the rep personnel have for sound experience selling the manufacturer's targeted customers with at least compatible product lines.

Income position — Ideally, a manufacturer should have a strong economic position with the rep firm as this position defines economic importance of the manufacturer to the rep. The manufacturer does not have to be the top income producer, but certainly should strive to be within the top three or four within a reasonable period of time, such as five years, presuming the manufacturer had almost no position in the territory prior to recruiting the rep. However, a precise fit in the rep's product and service package is a more imperative need than major economic position.

Successorship planning — To help assure continuity of the rep firm, owners should have a successorship plan in place, particularly if they are approaching the retirement age bracket. Many reps choose not to provide for continuity of the firm, but prefer just to start working at a reduced pace, then retire. At the retirement date, they may still represent a number of manufacturers who then have to go out and find a new rep. This is a very unattractive scenario for manufacturers, as invariably the rep who slows down loses market share for the manufacturers represented.

The bottom line is that having as clear a picture of what a rep should be to be highly productive for a manufacturer is the fundamental foundation step to searching for and recruiting the best available rep in a given territory.

THE SEARCH FOR TOP PERFORMING REPS

The search philosophy — It is essential that a meticulous and intensive search program be undertaken if a manufacturer is to achieve maximum market share inherently possible given the manufacturer's profile. Each territory has a defined rep population with varying degrees of compatibility with any given manufacturer. The basic philosophy one should use is that there is one best available rep for a manufacturer in a given territory (we use the term "available" because the best rep in absolute terms may not be available to a new manufacturer for a variety of reasons). If a manufacturer does not find that one best available rep, achievable market share in that territory will drop by varying degrees in accordance with the decreased compatibility of the selected rep. As an example, if a manufacturer had 20% share of a given market nationally, their shares from maximum to minimum in the various territories across the United States could well range from near 0 to over 40%. Presuming there is no unique commercial situation such as one truly outstanding account in the over 40% share territory, that one territory could well define what the maximum current market share is available to the manufacturer provided they have the right rep in that territory.

Based on the above philosophy, here is a search process that has been successfully followed by many manufacturers.

THE SEARCH PROCESS

As search consultants, we employ the following multi-step approach in conducting a search program:

Determine market priorities — This is the output of a manufacturer's planning which carefully defines markets and market niches by priorities along with the key essentials for success in each target. This framework is required in order that the rep profile will be totally compatible with the manufacturer's market priorities.

Target the territories and markets — If a manufacturer has an extensive number of territories needing rep coverage, priorities for the most important areas should be established. Care should be taken not to recruit so many reps that the manufacturer's support capabilities will be overloaded.

Define the opportunity in each territory, the investment required and the expected return — This simply means that no stone should be left unturned in high-potential territories. In territories where the opportunity is truly minimal, a manufacturer should actually consider leaving the territory uncovered and handled on an exception basis by reps in adjoining territories. The key is to allocate time, money and other resources to the territories where the best return can be achieved.

Identify prospective rep candidates — Generally, there is no single source for the names of all rep candidates in a given territory that might be compatible with the given manufacturer. This means that multiple sources should be used. Historically, manufacturers used four primary sources, namely:

- Asking key customers whom they would suggest.
- Rep, industry and other directories.
- Networking with their existing and other reps.
- Obtaining rep names from manufacturers of compatible products.

Other possible sources of rep names for a given territory include:

- Reps of competitors.
- Distributors (if the product line is sold by reps through distributors).
- Advertising (however, most companies generally do not succeed with advertising simply because the best available rep tends not to read the "help wanted" ads).
- Meeting prospective candidates at trade shows.
- The Internet. The Net is an emerging vehicle for finding reps. However, as of the end of 1999, there are significant limitations as this data source has yet to develop in a readily available manner.

Rep search firms. The really effective search firms will follow a process similar to that described here. Others will rely solely on a database they've developed. However, all databases are historic and do not necessarily represent all of the rep firms existing at the time a manufacturer conducts a new search.

Setting rep search firms aside for a minute, a successful candidate search program will invariably include a combination of the above sources. Our search practice uses our own database, but always complements it with searches in the most currently available directories, networking with reps, developing a list of compatible manufacturers and finding out their reps and looking at competitor's reps. Use of the Internet, and even helping sales personnel create a new rep firm are also occasional tools.

Upon completing a good search effort for candidates in a given territory, prospects may number less than 10 for some very narrow industries. More typically, 20 to 30 candidates will be found and in some industries, 50 or more prospects should be contacted. For example, in recent searches we have conducted in Illinois and Wisconsin for the manufacturer of plastic components, we located and contacted over 50 representatives in each territory, each one having some compatibility with our client.

Mail, Fax or E-mail a data package to the reps — This is simply to transfer information about the manufacturer to the rep candidate. This is not to replace use of the telephone but primarily to complement the next step, which would be the critically important telephone pursuit. The data package sent to the rep should include the history of the manufacturer, primary markets targeted, range of the products and applications, a definition of the territory and a statement as to whether or not there is established business in the territory. The amount of existing business that would be turned over to a new rep is best left to verbal discussions.

Provide relentless telephone pursuit — Another critical philosophy should be introduced at this step. It will be making the assumption that the rep a manufacturer really wants is not looking for a new manufacturer to represent. The truly outstanding reps are extremely busy. Typically, they will not be looking to add new manufacturers at the time a given manufacturer is searching for a rep. Therefore, these reps typically turn off inquiries from new manufacturers for representation and may even do it brusquely. However, once a rep candidate's attention is gained and the rep recognizes a uniquely compatible manufacturer, the addition of that manufacturer to the rep's lines normally becomes a priority to the rep.

Most reps realize that they have a number of lines that may no longer fit their primary objectives. Therefore, dropping several marginal lines and taking on a new line that really fits yields a handsome payback to the rep. As a result of our experience in rep search, we have established a minimum of five telephone follow-ups to the original data package sent to the reps in order to gain their attention. As a result of this aggressive follow-up, we typically reach a key owner of at least 90% to 95% of all reps originally listed in our candidate research.

Conduct the telephone interview — Once the rep's attention and interest is piqued, the rep owner will willingly spend whatever time is required on the telephone to gain a minimum transfer of information that might suggest a personal interview. Information that is generally given without reservation by reps during this telephone interview include the history of the business, current ownership, biographic sketches and tenures of all selling personnel, the territory they cover, markets and market niches targeted, major customers in the territory and any other information the rep feels could put them in a strong position with the manufacturer. These interviews should then be reduced to a series of reports on each rep candidate followed by a segregation of a rep's list into primary and secondary candidates.

Personally interview the top candidates — Personal interviews by the manufacturer are essential to not only gain the clinical information discussed above, but also to gain a feeling of the personal characteristics of the rep, the personal chemistry that results from the initial interview and a definition of the degree of interest by the candidate. Once personal interviews are completed, the manufacturer may then conduct a follow-up interview with the best of the candidates, meeting all sales personnel as well. At that time, the decision can be made on the recruitment.

The bottom line is to "make haste slowly" in the entire process. Once a rep is recruited, it may take two years or more for a manufacturer to find out that it was not a good selection. Lost opportunities by such a selection far outweigh any costs for doing an intensive search program that we have described. Following a search process that fits the uniqueness of a company and the industry in which it operates will result in highly successful rep recruitments and an optimization of market share achievement in the territory.

CHAPTER VII

QUID PRO QUOS OF THE REP-MANUFACTURER RELATIONSHIP

There are many factors that impact the profit making potential of the rep-manufacturer relationship. This chapter will present the *quid pro quos* generally accepted by reps and manufacturers as the support each party needs to provide the other if their mutual growth objectives are to be achieved. As two articles published in *Agency Sales Magazine* (October and November, 1996) directly presented these tradeoffs, this chapter comprises both articles.

**PART I —
EXPECTATIONS THAT REPS HAVE OF MANUFACTURERS**

During one of our seminars on the rep-manufacturer relationship, the president of a manufacturing company raised his hand and asked, "Why should we pay our rep a commission when they did absolutely nothing to get the order?" Last year, during a seminar at the Madison campus of the University of Wisconsin, a rep who was a member of a panel commented, "We do not tell manufacturers the names of the other manufacturers we represent, as it really is none of their business."

Both the president's question and the rep's comment reflect a clear lack of understanding of what is required for a highly-productive, long-term relationship between manufacturers and independent sales representatives. The most fruitful relationships are based on some very basic ingredients including a precise fit with each other, common objectives, mutual respect, complete openness in communications, and a clear understanding of the quid pro quos necessary for mutual success. If relationships have these ingredients and the partners approach their relationships in a win-win situation, a major competitive advantage may be gained by both parties in their targeted markets.

In the example of the aforementioned company president, the individual clearly did not understand all of the tradeoffs in the relationship. Reps perform many tasks for a manufacturer without receiving a single dollar in compensation. For example, they may do a rather complete selling job on a project including gaining a price premium only to lose it to a competitor because their manufacturer could not meet a customer's needed shipping date. Despite having done a rather total selling job, the rep does not get a penny. The same is true for the missionary effort a rep performs on behalf of a manufacturer, time spent in trying to resolve problems between the manufacturer and the customer, promotion of the manufacturer's products and myriad other selling and non-selling activities needed to develop a strong market position. Reps generally do not complain about non-payment of these activities as they are part of the quid pro quos of the relationship. Manufacturers should not complain about paying a commission for an "over-the-transom" order — as long as the rep is routinely a clear producer.

The aforementioned rep demonstrated that he did not understand the differences between rights and responsibilities. The independent rep certainly has the right to act independently. However, as a number of rep associations so perfectly phrase it, the relationship between rep and manufacturer is one of interdependence. Each party needs to recognize the responsibilities they have to the other party. One of the most basic ingredients in this interdependence is the need of the manufacturer to clearly know and understand all other principals handled by the representative, backgrounds and experience on all sales personnel, and myriad other details about the representative. Without this information, the manufacturer cannot adequately judge how well the representative fits the manufacturers' needs. Fortunately, in both of our examples, discussions with the president of the manufacturing company and the rep owner helped them understand the quid pro quos necessary to develop a win-win situation, that is, a profitable, long-term relationship for *both* the manufacturer and the rep.

This is the first of two articles which develop some of the more important responsibilities that each party has to the other. This part focuses on typical responsibilities that manufacturers have to their reps. In the second article, we'll present typical responsibilities a rep agency has to the manufacturers it represents.

The manufacturer's responsibilities

The umbrella requirement, as suggested above, is the need for the manufacturer to recognize all of the quid pro quos required for a win-win situation over the long term. After all, any win-lose confrontation invariably develops into a lose-lose relationship. To put this into perspective, following are a number of primary responsibilities that a manufacturer has to their representatives in order to achieve this long-term, win-win relationship:

1. **Responsiveness to customers** — There is nothing else that is more fundamental for achieving long-term market objectives. The manufacturer should constantly look to the representative, as well as directly to customers, for feedback to constantly improve product, service and system offerings. This obviously requires responsiveness to rep needs as the rep is the primary conduit connecting manufacturers to their customers.

2. **Quality products** — Nothing is more basic for a manufacturer's long-term profitability than furnishing quality products. This was one of the clear conclusions presented in *The PIMS Principles*[2].

---

[2] Buzzell & Gale, *The PIMS Principles* (New York: The Free Press, 1987), page 103.

Many reps view high product quality as the major single ingredient for enhancing the image and reputation of their firm and the manufacturers they represent.

3. **Integrity in word** — This simply means that manufacturers must routinely make commitments to perform, then live up to these commitments, whether it is to customer or rep. The willingness to routinely make commitments and have a sense of urgency in living up to them clearly defines the organizational culture of successful companies. The commitment register covers all aspects of the business from simply returning telephone calls to on-time shipments to prompt resolution of problems. This is the type of organizational culture that weds customers to suppliers and develops long-term commitment by reps to their manufacturers.

4. **Fair commission rates and commission policies** — While there are times when special commission incentives should be offered, reps are fairly basic in their needs. Commission rates, as product pricing, are determined by the marketplace. Each industry typically defines a commission level that reps need if they are expected to do a complete selling job. A simple survey can quickly define this base commission level. In addition, reps have the right to expect totally professional handling of all commission payments and associated commission matters by the manufacturers they represent.

Relative to special incentives, there are situations where we believe higher than normal commission rates or special payment timing also results in win-win situations. One example is the need for missionary effort to either help a company get established in a territory where they have little presence or in the launching of a new product for a company already well-received in the territory. Substantially increasing the commission rate and perhaps even paying on receipt of order allows the rep to more rapidly recover the cost of their missionary selling efforts. These special incentives should last for a sufficient time to allow reps to more rapidly recover their missionary effort costs. The added incentive also provides greater insurance to the manufacturer that prompt market penetration, so necessary for competitive advantage, is achieved.

5. **Acceptance as a business partner** — Too often we see anti-rep cultures within manufacturing organizations. Reps are viewed as outsiders rather than critical business partners needed to help the manufacturer achieve both short- and long-term market objectives. The most productive long-term relationships are based on mutual respect and mutual support. The senior executives of any manufacturer have a clear responsibility for developing a clear understanding of the need for this type of win-win relationship and developing a rep-supportive culture throughout the firm. Anything less is essentially shooting oneself in the foot before the race is started.

6. **A total marketing job** — Many elements go into a sound marketing effort. Here are just a few of them:

- *A sound marketing plan fully communicated to the reps.* This requires a very sound feedback system with a rep network. As they are the conduit to the marketplace, reps are in a superb position to advise on product and service needs, both short- and long-term. The manufacturer should accumulate all of this micro input, convert it into a macro picture and develop the appropriate plan. The plan, which should contain clear objectives, sound product and market strategies and detailed programs, then needs to be clearly communicated to the rep sales force in order that they know how to productively invest their time in the manufacturer.

  One of the contradictions that we frequently see in rep-manufacturer relationships is a classic complaint by executives that "those reps keep telling us how to run our business!" Reps who are committed to success tend to be quite aggressive in presenting their feelings to manufacturers about what is required to achieve success in their territory. Many executives feel uncomfortable as they cannot shut reps up as easily as they can direct people. This is a clear and obvious weakness in the executive personality, as there is nothing more important in business life than sound feedback. The bottom line is that if a rep is not telling a manufacturer how they should be running their business, the rep is not living up to their responsibilities in the overall quid pro quo relationship.

- *Close-coupled advertising and promotional programs.* Even small manufacturers can achieve excellent mileage from programs geared to their size. The objective should be to develop not only a company image in the marketplace, but also to develop qualified sales leads. Manufacturers should not expect reps to develop all sales opportunities by themselves. Promotion is a joint responsibility. Reps develop very high levels of commitment to a manufacturer who has a well-planned advertising and promotional program that generates qualified leads. The plus for the manufacturer is that it allows the manufacturer to obtain detailed feedback from their reps on these qualified leads and calculate the return on their investment in advertising and promotion.

- *Collateral material.* Included in this need are clear application and pricing data, competitive analyses, market analyses, success stories, organizational charts and contact points, and a variety of other materials any salesperson needs to be truly effective in the marketplace.

- *New products.* Many reps will not seriously consider establishing a relationship with a manufacturer if it is a total missionary effort. They want established product lines with a base of business from which they can receive an income stream while they further grow the business. Yet, as soon as they represent a manufacturer with established business, there is hardly any more motivating force to a representative than the manufacturer's introduction of quality new products. It gives the rep something new to talk about, that is, new values to offer their customers.

The above is not to suggest that high-performance reps will never take on a company that requires a total missionary effort in their territory. While it means that many reps will not touch this type of scenario, it will be rather rare when a manufacturer will not be able to find a well-matched rep willing to take on a company which has no established business. The primary reasons for a rep to consider such a missionary effort are fit, fit and fit. The rep sees that the manufacturer's products or services so perfectly fit what the rep is all about and the future appears so promising that a missionary effort is worth the investment.

- *Product Training.* We periodically hear a manufacturer complain that "our reps really don't know our product." This is one of a number of complaints that can generally be classified under that great old cartoon where Pogo once said, "We have met the enemy and they is us." If a rep network does not understand a manufacturer's product, the problems can invariably be traced to the manufacturer. The source of the problem can be one of a number of manufacturer-generated faults. Usually it's the result of not recruiting a sufficiently compatible representative combined with inadequate product training.

It should be clearly understood that reps rank product training highly in their expectations of manufacturers. In a major study by Dick Berry of the University of Wisconsin[3], Berry found that 88 percent of industrial reps surveyed ranked product training as very important to them. The rep's desire for product training is very easy to understand. With good training, they will be much more effective in their selling efforts and therefore generate a higher income for their invested effort.

---

[3] Berry, Dick. *Understanding and Motivating the Manufacturers' Agent* (Florence, KY, CBI Publishing Co. [now Van Nostrand Reinhold], 1981), p. 123

- *"No paper pushing."* Any sales organization should be evaluated on results. The two primary objectives are therefore sales performance (i.e., achieving penetration objectives) and quality feedback to help the manufacturer plan for the future. Too many manufacturers load up their sales organization with a bureaucratic flow of paperwork. While this is manageable (although not necessarily productive) with a direct sales organization, one must be very careful in the request for periodic or even special written reports by independent representatives. As they represent a number of different manufacturers, they tend not to have the time nor interest in generating bureaucratic paper flows. However, reps love to talk. We therefore urge that most feedback from reps be based on oral conversations. It not only takes advantage of the rep's communication preference, it also recognizes that oral dialogue is much more fertile in generating clear communications and sound understanding than a written document.

Fundamentals for success

The keys to outstanding success with independent reps are not complex. All it requires is that a manufacturer recognize that highly productive salespersons very favorably respond to a company that is highly sensitive to both customer and sales force needs. Reps do not need or even desire flamboyance in a company's plans and programs. They will respond best to a company that simply concentrates on the fundamentals needed for success in business; in other words, they love a well-managed company.

We suggest this focus on fundamentals need only be accompanied by one other managerial characteristic to achieve truly outstanding long-term success with reps. This would be the ability of all corporate executives to develop the necessary empathy with the selling position in order to feel what a sales rep feels, and in particular, an *independent* sales rep. Part of this should be the recognition that the rep typically needed is one who has already developed an outstanding track record, one who can manage the relationship with the customer on the manufacturer's behalf.

Corporate executives should put themselves in the shoes of the highly successful independent rep and ask two questions, namely: "What actions by the manufacturers I rep will really turn me on? What actions by these manufacturers will turn me off and cause me to divert my selling time to others?" If executives can develop this empathy, they'll have the answer to the great majority of all issues that arise between rep and manufacturer. This approach will clearly define the interdependency that exists between rep and manufacturer and provide each party with a clear path to a highly profitable, long-term relationship.

The steps a manufacturer needs to take to develop a truly committed rep network and therefore sharply increase their chances of long-term success in the marketplace are really not complex at all. Yet, many manufacturers do not achieve anywhere near the performance they would hope to achieve with independent reps. Invariably we have found the reasons to be sourced in the manufacturer's own failure to understand the basic elements in working successfully with independent reps. We trust that this article will help manufacturers better understand the quid pro quos necessary to develop a highly committed rep sales force and therefore sharply improve profitable penetration of their market targets. Next, we'll present the other side of this subject, namely the responsibilities independent reps have to the manufacturers they represent.

PART II —
EXPECTATIONS THAT MANUFACTURERS HAVE OF REPS

Above we presented a list of rational expectations that reps should have of manufacturers they represent. We also framed these expectations within the concept of an interdependent relationship that describes how each business partner should view the other. We now present a list of expectations that manufacturers should have of their reps. These expectations, however, must be prefaced by two caveats. First, there has to be a good match between rep and manufacturer. Second, the manufacturer must be supportive of the rep network. If a manufacturer has not met these two conditions for top rep performance, high expectations will not be realized.

The umbrella responsibility of reps to manufacturers they represent is to understand the quid pro quos in the relationship. In the first part of this chapter, we referred to a rep who advised an audience of manufacturers that he does not divulge the names of his other manufacturers to prospective principals. We responded by suggesting that this rep does not understand the interdependence between rep and manufacturer, as there is nothing more important to a manufacturer than understanding who are the other principals represented. How else can the manufacturer determine how well their company fits what the rep is all about? We find that the great majority of reps recognize this interdependence and therefore do not flaunt their independence. They recognize that outstanding long-term success with a manufacturer is achieved only by having common objectives and fully supporting their partner. With this framework in mind, following are the major responsibilities that we feel a rep has to the manufacturers they represent.

Commitment

Commitment to invest the necessary time, effort and expense to support the manufacturer at least to the level of income expected from that manufacturer. This commitment includes the mutual development and pursuit of objectives for penetrating the territory.

At times, we've listened to reps criticize the whole concept of objective setting as a bureaucratic time dissipater. Yet, considered objective setting entails a disciplined approach to market opportunities that many times becomes a positive, self-fulfilling prophecy. If objectives are established, plans and programs must be agreed upon to achieve these objectives. Add appropriate follow-up to monitor progress toward objectives and performance invariably is better than if no objectives had been set and business growth were simply left to chance.

The only other caveat we add is that the objectives should be stretch objectives when both manufacturer and rep have aggressive growth aspirations. By "stretch objectives," we mean setting targets for achievement that require high levels of performance by both parties. In today's highly competitive environment, high standards and aggressive pursuit of objectives is mandatory for survival, let alone growth.

Conversely, there is no sense setting stretch objectives when neither manufacturer nor rep has demonstrated the capability to achieve rapid growth. Both partners must therefore recognize their limitations and set more modest objectives. Even in this case, the very act of developing modest, mutual objectives improves the chances of achieving them.

Results

We define a successful relationship as one that achieves expected results for both parties. Manufacturers should therefore expect reps to produce a rational market share within a reasonable period of time. What is "rational" and what is "reasonable" is a function of many variables. In the case of a consumer products company where there is typically a quick turnaround of business, we have heard manufacturers and reps both set expectations of turning around a poorly performing territory to one that yields the manufacturer's national market share in less than six months. On the other hand, large capital equipment projects with long gestation periods may require several years of invested time on the part of the rep and manufacturer before the expected market share can be achieved. It is therefore important that the rep and the manufacturer agree upon these objectives (e.g., the above-stated objectives) and constantly assess progress toward them.

If the rep does not achieve expected market share within a reasonable period of time, both parties must reexamine the relationship to determine the cause for the shortfall. Perhaps it was simply a function of inflated objectives that had little chance of being attained. If so, objectives should be revised and share performance reassessed after an appropriate period of time.

On the other hand, non-attainment of expected share may be the result of a poor match between rep and manufacturer or poor support by one of the partners. If this is defined as the cause, the relationship should be carefully reexamined and agreements reached to resolve the problems or the relationship possibly terminated.

Maintaining a growth strategy

The executives of publicly held companies are invariably charged with the responsibility to grow that company. Success for these companies with independent reps means that the reps must also be growth oriented. This means common objectives, an essential requirement of long-term success.

Whereas the corporate executive typically cannot choose between growth and no growth strategies, the owners of independent rep firms have such a choice, as they are usually the sole owners of the business or at least have stock positions in excess of 50%. As a result, we frequently hear from reps that they have no intention of adding personnel. This is their right as independents, but it can also be a very clear statement to the manufacturer that the relationship is no longer functional.

A single-person firm has a limited number of hours available to sell for the manufacturers represented. If the market opportunity in the area permits growth and the individual rep does not expand, the manufacturer invariably will suffer loss of market share. We define this relationship as "dysfunctional" in that the objectives of the manufacturer remain in a growth mode while those of the individual rep have become "no growth" oriented, at least from a headcount addition perspective.

Once again, leaders of a publicly owned corporation do not have this choice. After all, what would the external board of directors say about a CEO who told the board and the stockholders that he has no intention of adding personnel to grow as he was quite satisfied with current sales and profitability? If the CEO were owner of more than half of the stock of the firm, he might be able to survive this statement, but he would invariably receive a lot of grief from the minority stockholders. If that CEO were not a holder of more than 50% of the company's stock, the other stockholders would more than likely ride him out of town on the proverbial rail.

Therefore, our advice to the single-person rep firm who is facing growth opportunities is "Grow." Otherwise, that person may well forfeit his or her right to represent growth-oriented manufacturers.

At times, we see a rep's staff declining from multi-person to single-person levels based on the owner's decision, either consciously or subliminally, to enter a lifestyle mode of repping rather than continue with the pressures of a growth mode. As mentioned above, this is certainly the rep's right. That is not disputed. However, by doing so, the rep's objectives have changed and are no longer compatible with the manufacturer's needs, namely an adequate headcount to provide intensive coverage of that trading area.

The senior executive of the manufacturer then has to recognize his responsibility to company stockholders and employee security is much greater than any loyalty to yesteryear's performance by a well-liked rep. There is only one clear ethical direction for the executive if the rep refuses to staff for growth — termination of the rep, or at least a contract modification that permits another rep to take advantage of the growth opportunity.

No competing lines

While we have occasionally seen a rep who handled directly competing lines without the manufacturers being aware of it, this is a major exception. We find the great majority of reps being highly professional and operating not only legally, but also ethically. Yet, there is always the danger that lines may be functionally competitive. We believe it is the rep's responsibility to discuss any functional competitiveness between lines represented between two principals and try to reach a win-win-win relationship.

This ethic also introduces the need for each rep to promptly alert a manufacturer any time one of the rep's other principals introduces a new product that is even partially competitive with an existing line.

Feedback

Reps should be selected for their intimate contacts with specific markets and customers targeted by the manufacturer in the rep's trading area. If a manufacturer's products or services do not precisely fit customer needs, the rep has a responsibility to advise the manufacturer. This feedback responsibility should also include feedback on competitive activity, changes in customer organizations that should be of interest to the manufacturer and all other data that would be prudent for a manufacturer to understand in order to better plan the future.

The most common complaint we hear from manufacturers when talking about reps is poor communication. Closer examination reveals it's more of a shortfall in form than substance. By this, we mean that reps generally are good at providing feedback verbally, but are much less so when it comes to reducing it to writing. Our advice to reps is to negotiate how feedback is to be conducted with each principal in order that expectations are rational and achievable by both.

Prompt announcement of changes in principals and key employees

The two characteristics of a rep that perhaps best define the compatibility of a rep with a manufacturer are the quality of principals represented and the capability of their sales personnel. If the rep has a change in either key sales personnel or principals represented, the rep should routinely advise the manufacturers they represent of these changes. It is similar to a manufacturer's responsibility to advise the rep of changes in the manufacturer's staffing, products and market priorities. The responsibility of advising them of changes is not an attempt by manufacturers to manage a rep's business. It is simply the type of open communication that is so vital to outstanding long-term success.

Investment in product training

This responsibility is very well shouldered by reps as long as they have a commitment to that manufacturer. Reps want product training in order to improve their chances of closing a sale and therefore get a better return for their invested dollar. If one has a rep who constantly puts off attending obviously needed training, we would suspect that the rep is not committed to the manufacturer.

Appropriate promotion

In this day and age, many reps have become marketers as well as salespersons. Part of their marketing work is to develop promotions for the products they represent. A major question becomes: "What is appropriate?" Here is where we counsel manufacturers to be less concerned about the "how" of promotion than the results achieved by their reps. Each successful rep achieves their success in a way compatible with the leanings of the rep personnel in that organization. We therefore suggest that manufacturers leave the "how to" up to the reps. However, we also suggest that reps should recognize the need to promote each principal's offerings and to use each manufacturer's promotional capabilities as they best fit what that rep firm is all about.

Some miscellaneous items

Assistance in collection problems — Holdups in payment of invoices are frequently the result of some minor stumbling blocks.

The rep is typically in a better position to define that stumbling block and the steps needed to resolve it than an accounts receivable clerk in the manufacturer's headquarters. We therefore feel that reps should provide assistance in collection problems with parameters agreed upon with the manufacturer they represent.

Proposal preparation and order write-ups — With today's computer capability and software programs, reps typically prefer to develop proposals themselves, as this puts them almost completely in control of the proposal process. We suggest more and more reps jump on this bandwagon and request such software programs from the manufacturers they represent.

Summary

The most successful and enduring relationship between manufacturers and reps is one based on rather simple fundamentals. The foundation is a precise fit between rep and manufacturer, common objectives and a commitment to support each other. Then, all that is required is a routine auditing process to make sure that problems are promptly identified and resolved, opportunities are quickly pinpointed and penetrated and course adjustments in the relationship are made as they are defined necessary. This is just simple, good business practice.

There are really no complex or magical aspects of outstanding rep-manufacturer relationships. Exercising some good common sense, respect for your partner and a commitment to a win-win relationship will do it. This is even true at that point in time when the objectives of one or both parties change to the extent that the relationship should be terminated. Both parties should leave the relationship with nothing but fond memories of a great run.

CHAPTER VIII

EVALUATING AND ADJUSTING THE RELATIONSHIP

Evaluating the relationship

There is a continuing need by both reps and manufacturers to constantly evaluate the progress of their relationship towards achievement of their objectives. There is a constantly changing scenario that reps and manufacturers face not only in the marketplace but in their own organizations. The primary need is the objective assessment of performance in each rep's territory relative to the marketplace opportunities and the objectives that both rep and manufacturer agree upon. If there is a performance shortfall that clearly shows that the rep is not achieving the level of performance that is rationally expected for the territory, manufacturers will routinely find that the shortfall is due to any one of four reasons, namely:

1. The rep channel design developed by the manufacturer does not provide adequate coverage for all targets.
2. The selection process of the manufacturer recruited reps who insufficiently matched their needs.
3. Poor support by the manufacturer turned their rep's attention to other companies they represented.
4. Objectives of either the manufacturer or the rep firm changed and sharply reduced compatibility.

Let's look at each cause:

Poor channel design — An example of this was Glegg Water

Conditioning's early rep recruitment program, which sought to find the most technically qualified rep in water treatment and then assign all market opportunities to the rep. In essence, this is the design of a sales channel on the basis of product capability rather than market. The result is that Glegg recruited some outstanding reps but outstanding only in specific markets and not others.

For example, one outstanding rep was a specialist in ultra-pure water and did an excellent job in an industry (e.g., semiconductor chip manufacturing) that had a high demand for ultra-pure water in the manufacturing process. However, this rep did not understand the power industry and, therefore, was not productive in covering major accounts that needed water treatment for boiler demineralization. This problem is an example of poor channel design rather than poor rep selection. Once this was recognized, Glegg quickly extracted the power market from the rep's contract and established a separate rep who concentrated on the power market. The original rep continued to be highly successful in its niche.

A poor selection process — This gets back to the chapter on rep selection. The search process for independent reps must be carefully planned, as a successful rep will usually not change the way they are conducting business or make any major change in their market mix for a new manufacturer. It is, therefore, imperative that the manufacturer selects a rep that is a precise extension of what the manufacturer is all about.

Poor support — Reps will allocate their time among the manufacturers they represent according to not only gross commission dollars but, even more importantly, the commission dollars obtained for their invested time and effort. This means a manufacturer that is well matched with a rep must also make that rep's selling job easy through proper support. The previous chapter discussed these expectations in some detail.

Changing objectives — Change is obviously inevitable. Markets change, processes within markets change, competition changes, manufacturers change and reps change. At times, a manufacturer and their reps will change in the same direction to meet new market needs. However, as often as not, objectives of a rep will change in a different direction than that of a manufacturer. A rep may elect to go into manufacturing, which can be a major dissipation of time. The rep may elect to invest heavily in a new market of no interest to a manufacturer. A rep may elect to make a transition from an aggressive, growth posture to one where a comfortable lifestyle is more important than growth. Any one of these changes can be detrimental to the relationship and suggests the relationship be changed.

Following are several tools that can be used by manufacturers to evaluate the relationship in terms of the overall relationship with the entire rep network and that of individual reps:

1. **A rep council** — A rep council is a small body of individuals selected from a number of representatives (typically four to six) who periodically meet with the manufacturer to discuss a manufacturer's problems, opportunities and recommended solutions to issues they face in common in the marketplace. In times of difficult business relationships, meetings may be scheduled as often as quarterly. More typically, these meetings are semiannual or annual.

Attending from the manufacturer should be the senior operating officer (e.g., CEO, president or division manager) and the major functional managers (e.g., V. P. of engineering, director of operations, controller and marketing V. P.).

The agenda should be developed by both parties and sent to the other party before the meeting. The meetings, which typically last one day, should then be held in a fast-moving, bottom-line oriented, decision-making style in which issues are presented, alternative solutions addressed and decisions made on the direction to be taken. As the senior management team from the manufacturer is there as well as key individuals from each of a number of reps, at least conceptual solutions can be agreed upon with the details to be worked out shortly thereafter. Rep councils are a superb mechanism for companies to use to obtain very objective feedback on what is required to be successful in the marketplace.

2. **Rep audit** — The rep audit is an auditing process whereby an independent auditor (i.e., one with both general management and rep sales management experience) conducts the audit process. It entails interviewing one or more key individuals at each rep firm concerning that firm's appraisal of the manufacturer's capabilities to succeed in the marketplace and properly support the rep. Upon completing the interviews of the rep network (or at times, a sampling of the rep network), the auditor will be able to put together a very sound picture of key strategic and operating issues faced by the manufacturer in the marketplace and sound steps that can be taken to resolve them.

Through the interview, the auditor will also obtain the current characteristics of each individual rep firm, in order to determine how compatible each rep is currently with the manufacturer's objectives. The auditing process we have used typically uncovers many relationships between rep and manufacturer that are no longer compatible or have never been compatible from the inception. The following table shows the varying degrees of compatibility uncovered during the audit process for 24 manufacturers in a period from the mid to late 1990s.

REP/MANUFACTURER COMPATIBILITY RATINGS
Compiled from Rep Audits for 24 Manufacturers
by Novick & Associates, Inc.

	Compatible	Marginal	Not Compatible	Total
No. of Rep Firms	202	158	120	480
% of Total	42.1%	32.9%	25.0%	100.0%

3. **Other feedback tools** — There are other feedback tools that manufacturers should use to constantly appraise the progress of their relationship with their rep sales force. These include:

- Regional managers' reports
- Customer visits to the plant
- Visits to customers
- Trade shows
- Industry publications
- An open organizational culture that encourages rep feedback

ADJUSTING OR TERMINATING THE RELATIONSHIP

The relationship between rep and manufacturer should be routinely monitored throughout the year. In addition, there should be specific checkpoints where a more formal assessment of the progress of the relationship is made and in the event of shortfalls, steps taken to correct the shortfalls. Again, most performance failures are attributed to any one or more of the four reasons previously cited. Let's again look at each one and suggest what steps can be taken to resolve the problem:

1. **Poor channel design** — This is the case where the rep was very compatible with a manufacturer's objectives for a specific market but not other markets. The answer is simple, adjust the contract, letting the vertical-market-oriented rep keep the market that they target while reassigning markets not covered by the rep to other reps who specialize in those markets.

2. **A recruited rep who does not match the manufacturer's needs** — This is simply an error in the selection process for both rep and manufacturer. The bottom line is that if a relationship is not successful for one of the parties, typically it is not rewarding for the other party. These relationships should be terminated and a new rep recruited.

3. **Poor support has demotivated a rep sales force** — Quite frequently, we have found that a manufacturer simply does not support their reps at a level even close to the support given by the other manufacturers working with that rep. Typically, that rep will then reallocate time that should be spent with one manufacturer to the others. It, therefore, becomes critical for that manufacturer to understand the shortfalls in their support, make a commitment to sharply upgrade their performance and aggressively attack and resolve the deficiencies.

4. **Changing objectives** — Changing objectives by either of the two firms in the relationship may result in that relationship no longer being compatible. In this situation, rep and manufacturer should face up to it and agree on a separation. However, there are times when contract adjustments are the preferred solution. This can be a change in the agreed-upon markets to be targeted, assignments based on specific customer targets or possibly even a modification of the territory. Each case should be examined based on its own merit and win/win solutions developed.

THE TERMINATION

When the relationship between manufacturer and a rep is no longer profitable, invariably it is not profitable for both parties. The proper step for both parties is to recognize this situation and amicably terminate the relationship. Manufacturers should be professional in their approach to a deteriorating relationship, addressing the problem with their reps on a win/win basis, documenting all of the concerns and steps to be taken and then, if a turnaround is not achieved, to terminate the relationship for cause.

One of the major issues on terminations is the rights of the representative upon being terminated. Care needs to be exercised that their successful contribution over the tenure of the relationship is fairly rewarded. Many contracts with reps include a 30-day termination period whereby no commission credit is given reps for any orders received beyond 30 days. Now, certain industries will extend this period and the other conditions in a number of ways in order to give the rep a fair termination agreement.

CHAPTER IX

CASE EXAMPLES

Following are examples of four different companies reflecting four different scenarios of success with independent reps.

Fisher Controls, a large company committed totally to reps

Fisher Controls is a major manufacturer of instrumentation and controls, primarily for the process industries. They are located in Marshalltown, Iowa and have sales well over one billion dollars worldwide. The firm is owned by Emerson Electric, one of the most financially astute corporations in the world.

Fisher has used independent reps exclusively for sales in the United States and Canada since their inception. Their sales now approach one billion dollars annually in this major territorial market and again, it is all through independent reps.

Fisher uses one rep firm for each trading area. Their largest rep, Puffer-Sweiven, in Houston, Texas, has sales around $200 million of which around 70% is Fisher. The other representatives' sales average around 90% from Fisher. This very high economic dependence on Fisher resulted in John Weekley, former vice president of sales, to classify the network as being a "pseudo-direct sales force." (Mr. Weekley is now president of Proconex, Fisher's rep in Philadelphia.)

The current Fisher rep is definitely of the high-tech character. Each firm develops their business to meet local needs which include not only the sale of instrumentation and control, but also the analysis, design, sale, installation and service of complete systems.

As Fisher looks at the millennium market scenario, the name of the game requires a company to offer leading-edge technology, a systems approach, local service and an ability to adapt products, systems and services to local needs. In addition, a global perspective is now needed, as many domestic customers have global interests. Fisher Controls continues to believe in the rep approach. The major reason offered by Joe Urbanek, vice president of Fisher-Rosemount North America, is that their independent reps are in a much better position to assure customer satisfaction on a local basis, as total accountability and authority are vested in each rep's independent business. This type of local flexibility is typically unavailable in direct sales organizations where decisions are usually made by the company on a macro rather than micro basis.

The key lesson from Fisher is that size of a company's sales are simply not a reason for going direct. Marketplace demands on the large company can be better met in many respects by an independent rep sales force, similar to Fisher's.

Hewlett-Packard, a large company using reps to complement direct selling

This pertains to the medical products segment of HP's business. It is a profit center with sales of $1.3 billion, with a primary focus on capital equipment for larger hospitals, that is, those institutions with 200 or more beds.

In the mid-1990s, HP found that while they had excellent coverage of the larger hospital market, their coverage of small hospitals and the many other medical establishments needing capital equipment was very weak. The poor economics of direct coverage of the smaller accounts resulted in this weak coverage.

HP, therefore, developed an "alternative sales channel" group. Their objective was to develop a supplemental channel of independent reps to cover these secondary markets. By 1999, sales of this organization accounted for nearly 20% of HP's sales in the United States and an even higher percentage overseas.

Many billion-dollar companies face similar scenarios. The company may have one or two primary market targets, which are effectively covered by a direct sales organization. However, that sales force typically does not adequately cover secondary markets or even marginal trading areas for primary market targets. Here is where an independent rep structure can be developed to provide a perfect complement to direct selling.

Glegg Water Conditioning, Inc. (now GE-Glegg Water Technologies), a medium-sized company committed to reps

Robert Glegg, CEO, started his company as an entrepreneur in 1978. His primary focus was on the power industry, where he offered high-quality water treatment equipment to Canadian and U.S. customers. Headquartered in Guelph, Ontario, Mr. Glegg made the appropriate marketing decision that their primary target was the U.S. market because of its enormous size compared to the Canadian market. Expansion into international markets soon followed.

Their initial channel concept was to use reps for the power market in the U.S. They then targeted two additional markets, namely the pharmaceutical and electronic industries. In the late 1990s, separate rep channels were set up for each of these two specialized markets. The result was Glegg had as many as three reps in a given territory, each one focused on one of the targets. In more marginal trading areas, or in the case of a truly unusual rep, one rep might be used for all three markets.

This strong channel design concept followed up by the recruitment of highly compatible reps was supported by the company's superb capability to build a quality product and ship it in a timely manner. Glegg Water Conditioning reached the hundred-million-dollar sales level in the late 1990s. Within this scenario, there was occasional direct coverage resulting primarily from extremely large users developing sole-source agreements with Glegg. There were a minimum number of such examples as Glegg continued their commitment to reps.

As a company expands its market targets, extreme care is needed in channel design planning and development. Taking advantage of rep specialization in vertical markets, such as exhibited by Glegg Water Conditioning, is one of the highly successful channel strategies available to manufacturers and service providers.

Buckeye Manufacturing Company, a small company growing with reps

Buckeye, a small pressure vessel and tank manufacturer in Springboro, Ohio, was founded in 1963. It is currently owned by Dick Macaulay, son of the founder. Until the late '90s, sales were handled by two individuals within the firm who also performed other functions. There was no dedicated selling effort.

Dick Macaulay recognized that if he were to achieve his objectives for the company, that is, to become a major factor in his targeted markets, he needed to establish a strong independent rep channel. He initially recruited three reps, but only one of them performed successfully.

Macaulay's problem was namely insufficient time and insufficient experience in conducting the extremely precise search and selection process that is needed by a small company to find well-matched reps. The two non-performing reps simply were not a good match with Buckeye's needs.

After adopting the search process described earlier, the next three reps recruited by Macaulay exhibited success in the relationship. Each of these representatives were well established, with experienced, professional sales staffing and a strong focus on engineered applications for liquid processing and handling in the process industries, characteristics essential in a rep to be successful with Buckeye's product lines. Macaulay is now working with his minimum rep network as he recognizes the need not to overextend the company's capability to support his rep network. He will recruit additional reps only when he and the existing reps feel confident further territorial expansion can be undertaken and new reps ably supported.

Most small companies, such as Buckeye, are usually faced with only one viable channel opportunity, namely the use of the independent reps. The variable expense of reps permits small companies the luxury of obtaining outstanding sales coverage, while not having to pay up-front money as with a direct sales force. In the case of Buckeye, they were able to recruit top-level reps despite their small size. This is partly the result of reps enjoying a direct relationship with a president/owner, such as Dick Macaulay, who has conveyed a long-term commitment to independent reps and to highly effective support of them. We believe that Buckeye Fabricating has established a channel strategy that will help Macaulay achieve his objectives of growing his company to be a major factor in his industry.

SUMMARY

Again, this booklet is designed to help the reader obtain an overview of the independent sales representative, a sales channel that best matches the characteristics needed by most manufacturer's in a sales channel as we begin the 21st century. The need has never been greater for a sales force to be systems-oriented with long tenure with key customers that allows them to be relationship managers. Also needed is the flexibility to adapt product, service and systems offerings to local needs and a large headcount of qualified sales personnel with vertical market specialization. These are major advantages offered by a properly selected independent rep sales force that can offer companies, whether they be small, medium or large in size, competitive advantage in the marketplace.

For more detailed reading on the subject, we suggest the third edition of *Selling Through Independent Reps* by Harold J. Novick, and published by the American Management Association's publishing division, AMACOM, copyright 2000, New York, New York. A detailed listing of various sources of information on independent reps may also be obtained through the Manufacturers' Representatives Educational Research Foundation (MRERF) in Geneva, Illinois. For a rather exhaustive list of materials on the rep/manufacturer relationship, one may also contact the Manufacturers' Agents National Association (MANA) in Laguna Hills, California.

Harold J. Novick is president of Novick & Associates, Inc., a general management and industrial marketing consulting firm that specializes in helping companies increase sales and profits by using independent reps and distributors. His clients include Babcock & Wilcox, DuPont, Mitsubishi, Monsanto and Unisys. Previously, Mr. Novick served as president of the Permutit Company, Inc., and Garry Manufacturing Company, and as group executive at Research-Cottrell. He has also held senior sales and marketing positions at Joy Manufacturing Company and Westinghouse. He is the author of the two previous editions of this book, and his articles have appeared in *Industry Week*, *Business Marketing*, *Management Review*, *Agency Sales* and many other magazines. He lives in Pittstown, New Jersey.